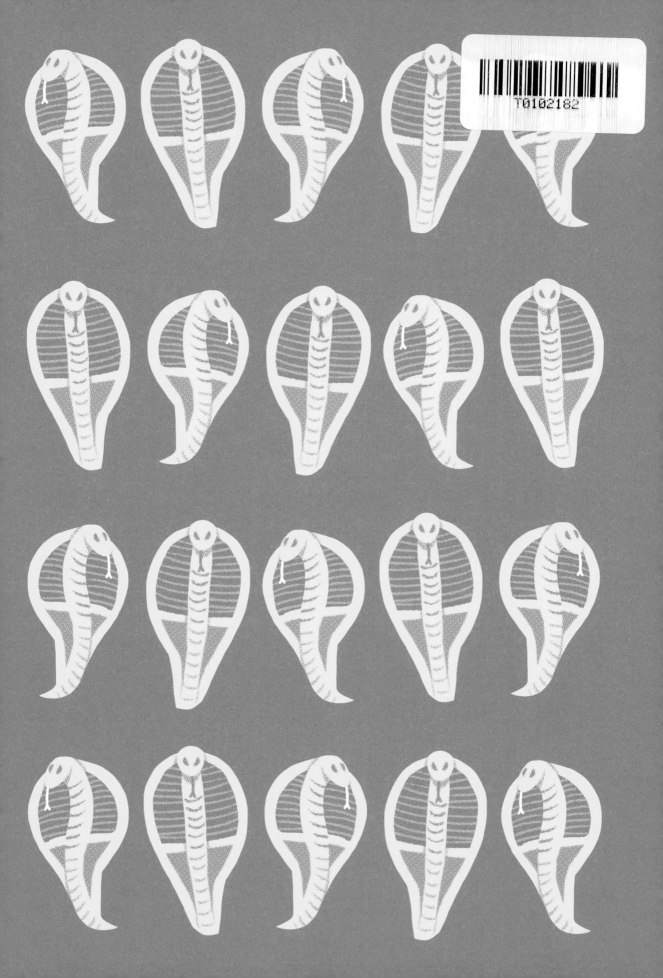

For Charlotte – C.N.

To Lucca and Vicente – G.K.

CLEOPATRA

TELLS ALL!

Chris Naunton

Illustrated by
Guilherme Karsten

CONTENTS

AT THE MUSEUM

UNIDENTIFIED PTOLEMAIC QUEEN
200–30 BCE

This statue is thought to represent one of the queens from the Ptolemaic royal family, the last dynasty of ancient Egypt. She holds a cornucopia—an object shaped like a horn—which was a symbol of abundance and wealth in ancient times.

Children, look closely at her appearance—do you recognize the hair style? It's thought she might have been one of the seven Cleopatras, who were queens in Ptolemaic Egypt. "Cleopatra" means "glory of her father" in Macedonian.

"Unidentified?!"
"One of the seven?!"
"Glory of her father?!"
Of course it's me—I am THE Cleopatra!

I'm the most famous —Cleopatra VII. And I'm famous in my own right, thank you very much.

When you've calmed down, can I get a selfie?

HELLO, I'M CLEOPATRA VII...

PEOPLE OF THE WORLD!

You may know me as Julius Caesar's girlfriend. But I prefer to be known for my achievements. The problem is, even if you're the pharaoh of Egypt, you can't always control who writes history. So I thought a letter from me to you would be a nice way for me to set the record straight.

I descend from a long line of leaders in the Ptolemaic Dynasty. I am highly intelligent and an excellent communicator (which can't be said for all world leaders). Most importantly, I know how to get things done.

Call me "Cleopatra VII" if you like, but "Cleo" is fine with me. I know I'm more than a number.

Cleo xoxo

#make it happen!

MAKE IT HAPPEN

Being pharaoh involves a surprising amount of paperwork—contracts, tax notices, etc. I quickly learned how to delegate tasks to other people. I dictated my orders to a scribe who wrote them out on papyrus. Then I signed them by writing the Greek word "ginesthoi," which means "make it happen!"

ONCE UPON A TIME IN...
ALEXANDRIA

"Where are all the **pyramids**?" I hear you ask. We're not in the desert any more, kiddos...

INVADED BY THE GREEKS

My family—the Ptolemies (that's pronounced "Toll-om-mees")—are from Macedonia in ancient Greece. You see, in 525 BCE Egypt was invaded by the Persians. Then Egypt was conquered by the Macedonian king, Alexander the Great. My story starts with him.

ALEXANDER'S NEW TOWN

Alexander the Great arrived in Egypt in 332 BCE. Wherever he conquered a new land, he built a city. Egypt already had a capital city, called Memphis. But Alexander wanted a city like the ones he had at home, with streets in straight lines and a cooler climate. So he built a new city on the coast where the River Nile meets the Mediterranean Sea and named it "Alexandria" after himself. Humble, or what?

A WONDER OF THE WORLD

The lighthouse on the Island of Pharos is an enormous 440 ft tall, and was built in c. 280 BCE of different tiers of marble. The light is focused by gigantic polished mirrors—technological wizardry by our standards! The only taller human-made buildings at this point in time are Egypt's own pyramids at Giza.

SEASIDE HUB

Alexandria couldn't be more different from Memphis—it enjoys cool sea breezes instead of hot, dusty winds; it rains in the winter instead of flooding in the summer; and there are always lots of boats coming and going, bringing people from all over the world. It's got a cool, international vibe.

HOW I BECOME PHARAOH

I come from a **long** line of Ptolemies and Cleopatras, which is why we need **numbers** after our names (see page 47). We start out **Greek** and become more Egyptian as time goes on...

1 **ALEXANDER THE GREAT DIES**

My great, great, great, great, great, great-grandfather, Ptolemy I Soter, is a general in Alexander's army. When Alexander unexpectedly dies in 323 BCE, Ptolemy steps in to "help"—by ruling Egypt.

2 **PTOLEMY SNATCHES ALEXANDER'S BODY**

Alexander the Great's body is sent back to Macedonia in a burial chariot called a "catafalque." Ptolemy I intercepts the chariot and diverts it to Memphis. He claims Alexander's dying wish is to be buried in Egypt—and people believe him!

MEMPHIS

Macedonia

3 PTOLEMY I TAKES THE THRONE

Ptolemy I builds a temple for Alexander the Great's body and turns it into a tourist attraction. There is no doubt in anyone's mind that the Ptolemies RULE. The Ptolemaic Dynasty is born and Egypt gets a brand new king.

COME VISIT!

ALEXANDER THE GREAT SARCOPHAGUS

SAVE 10%

4 9 PTOLEMIES LATER...

Fast forward a few centuries to 81 BCE. Ptolemy IX is the king of Egypt. His brother, Ptolemy X (my family has no imagination when it comes to names), is already dead. Unlike the ancient Egyptians, the Ptolemies don't let women inherit property, let alone a kingdom. So when Ptolemy IX dies without a male heir, we are forced to adapt.

5 A FAMILY FEUD BEGINS

Ptolemy IX's daughter Berenice takes the throne and calls herself "Berenice Cleopatra." She is both Ptolemy IX's daughter and the wife of his brother, the late Ptolemy X. In keeping with family tradition, she agrees to marry her stepson and nephew, Ptolemy XI. Unfortunately they don't get along...

13

DOUBLE MURDER!!

Ptolemy XI thinks that he should be the king, not Cleopatra Berenice. So within 3 weeks of their wedding, he murders her and takes the throne for himself. But the Alexandrian people disapprove of his behavior, drag him to the gymnasium and kill him in revenge. Gory!

7 WE FIND A NEW HEIR

Because Cleopatra Berenice was the last of the true Ptolemies and had no children, our dynasty is at risk of ending. We need a new heir, and fast! The crown is given to a young man who is the son of Ptolemy IX and a little-known woman now living in Syria. Meet Ptolemy XII Auletes—my father ("auletes" means "the flute-player").

8 EGYPT HAS A NEW KING AND GOD

Ptolemy XII wants to reassure everyone that he is the rightful ruler of Egypt. He changes his name to "Ptolemy Theos Philopator Philadelphos Neos Dionysos" which means "Ptolemy, the Father-Loving, Brother/Sister-Loving God, the New Dionysos." The Greek god Dionysos is popular with Alexandrians, and is also linked to the Egyptian god Osiris. Everyone is happy!

⑨ ROME IS NOT HAPPY

The Alexandrians might be happy with their new ruler but Rome is not... Technically speaking, the kingdom of Egypt was gifted to the Roman Empire in Ptolemy X's will. Ptolemy XII gives away half of Egypt's yearly income to Rome's 3 rulers—Pompey the Great, Crassus and Julius Caesar.

POMPEY

CRASSUS

JULIUS CAESAR

⑩ YET MORE FAMILY MURDERS

My father goes on a business trip to Pompey's villa in Rome—and decides to stay. My older sister makes herself queen and murders her husband only 1 week after their wedding (apparently he was very vulgar). So poor Dad has to have her executed #awkward. When my father eventually dies, we are all surprised it is from natural causes.

⑪ I BECOME PHARAOH

I am 18 when I become the ruler of Egypt. I am the coregent, or joint-ruler, with my younger brother Ptolemy XIII, who is only 10 years old. The rulers of the Roman Empire are our "guardians." The real story starts here...

THE REALITY OF RULING

Being the queen of Egypt sounds **wonderful**, I bet.
I'll let **you** weigh up the pros and cons:

Pro #1: THE ROYAL PALACE IS 5-STAR LUXURIOUS

The royal court in Alexandria is sumptuous to say the least. It's full of statues, sphinxes, and columns which are made from expensive stones like agate, marble, alabaster, onyx, lapis lazuli, and porphyry. But living in luxury comes at a cost...

Con #1: EGYPT HAS NO MONEY

Because my father felt so insecure about his position as king, he gave away a lot of money— mostly to the Romans. Along with this palace, I have inherited huge amounts of debt.

Pro #2: EGYPT IS ONE MASSIVE GRAIN STORE

The River Nile usually floods every summer, like clockwork. The flood water nourishes the land and food is really easy to grow. Full stomachs make for a happy population. However...

Con #2: FOOD IS RUNNING OUT

In recent years the floods have been less predictable. We are starting to run out of food...

Pro #3: I SHARE THE THRONE WITH MY LITTLE BROTHER

I am the coruler of Egypt along with my younger brother, Ptolemy XIII. It's a very effective way of protecting the family dynasty but also super weird because that also means...

Con #3: I AM MARRIED TO MY LITTLE BROTHER

Firstly—ewwww! Secondly, my brother is only 10 and knows very little about how to run a country. I decide to just ignore him—this turns out to be a mistake. Failing is learning, right?

QUEEN OF THE GEEKS

Power dressing can only take you so far in life. It was being a **total** geek that made me a world leader. Here are my **top five** geek girl tips:

TIP #1:
GET A GOOD EDUCATION

I am privileged enough to have had a private tutor, Philostratos, who taught me oration (how to give good speeches) and philosophy— two very important skills if you want to become a world leader.

TIP #2:
LEARN MULTIPLE LANGUAGES

I figure that if I want my subjects to like me and obey me, they'll probably pay more attention if I can speak their native language. I am fluent in Greek, Egyptian, Syrian, Arabian, and Ethiopian. Impressive, I know.

TIP #3:
EAVESDROP ON SCHOLARS

I often go in disguise to the Museion—a research center attached to the palace with lecture halls, laboratories, and guest rooms for visiting scholars. It's where famous academics including Archimedes and Euclid solved math and physics problems, and where the astronomer Aristarchus of Samos discovered that the Sun was the center of the solar system. There's so much to learn just by listening in on brainy conversations!

WHAT A COPY CAT!

How did our library in Alexandria become so packed full of scrolls? We've made it compulsory for all foreign ships that visit to hand over any scrolls they're carrying, for copying. It's not stealing, just borrowing.

ERATOSTHENES

TIP #4:
BE INSPIRED BY THE GODS

The Museion is also a temple to the muses—these are the Greek goddesses who we believe inspire ideas for poetry, literature, and art. Fun fact: "museion" is where you get the word "museum" from.

TIP #5:
LIVE NEXT DOOR TO THE BEST LIBRARY IN THE WORLD

The library inside the Museion is the biggest library in the ancient world! Conveniently for me, it's also right next door. Our first chief librarian, Eratosthenes, was so smart he calculated the Earth's circumference to an accuracy of a few hundred miles—and this is before calculators or the Internet!

HOW I GET BOOTED OFF THE THRONE

Despite my superior talents, my little brother still manages to remove me from the throne.

POWER PLAY

Ptolemy and his assistant Pothinus don't like me much and decide to get rid of me. The nerve! My family has a history of playing dirty, so I have actually prepared for this. I flee to Syria and organize my own army (being fluent in Syrian REALLY comes in handy). We march to Egypt, ready to fight back!

MY BROTHER'S BIG MISTAKE

Meanwhile, two Romans are having their own fight. One is called Pompey and the other one is Julius Caesar. Pompey goes on the run and turns up in Alexandria to ask my brother for help. Instead, my brother cuts Pompey's head off. Big mistake...

I FIND A FRIEND IN CAESAR

My brother is very pleased with himself. But when Julius Caesar arrives in Alexandria and is greeted with the head of Pompey, Caesar doesn't like it one bit—an Egyptian king has killed a Roman citizen! I am starting to see how Caesar and I could become friends...

I PLOT MY RETURN

If I can just get Caesar on my side, I am confident I'll be able to win over Egypt, too. The Egyptian people like me much more than they like Ptolemy. I speak to them in Egyptian, and one of the first things I did as queen was to accompany a new sacred Buchis bull after the old one died at the temple in Armant. Dedicated, or what?

My first boyfriend, JULIUS CAESAR

Everyone has a story about how they meet their first love—mine is more dramatic than most. It involves me going undercover to sneak back into my own palace...

FIRST, SOME BACKGROUND

I can see that Julius Caesar is fast becoming the most powerful man on Earth. I've thought about just messaging him, but decide it's better to talk face-to-face. My brother will kill me if he catches me back in Alexandria, so I make an elaborate plan...

OUR FIRST DATE

1 I leave the army camp in Pelusium and travel back to Alexandria on a nondescript little boat.

2 When I arrive at the palace, I make sure no one can see it is me. Some say I was rolled up in a carpet, others say in a bed-sack, or that I just wore a veil to conceal my face. WHATEVER—I manage to sneak all the way into Caesar's room.

3 I don't reveal who I am until I am standing right in front of Caesar himself. Surprise!

4 Apparently I have a very nice voice, so when I find myself in front of Caesar, I just start talking. He likes me right away and totally agrees with me that I should be reinstated as pharaoh! WHOOP! Job done.

ARE WE MARRIED?!

In ancient Egyptian culture, going steady means you're married. In ancient Rome, there has to be a ceremony. As far as I'm concerned, us dating means we're committed for life. I'm not sure Caesar is aware of this—he already has a wife...

ANCIENT POWER COUPLE

Julius and I are no ordinary couple. We're both politically savvy, we each rule large empires, and we have a shared love of power. That said, basic relationship advice still applies...

1 FIND SOME COMMON INTERESTS

As we all know, it's not enough to woo someone. To build a lasting relationship, you need to find some common interests. As well as both wanting to rule the world, Caesar and I have both recently been at war—Caesar with Pompey, and me with my brother/husband Ptolemy XIII. We also both love dressing in disguise—Caesar disguised his whole fleet of ships to sneak past Pompey to defeat him! We're a match made in heaven.

2 INTRODUCE THEM TO YOUR FAMILY

Soon after our first date, Caesar arranges a meeting between myself and Ptolemy where he reads out our dad's will, confirming that Ptolemy and I should rule Egypt together. The problem is, we have two other siblings: a sister called Arsinoe and ANOTHER Ptolemy (XIV!). Being the generous guy that he is, Caesar gives them Cyprus to go off and rule. Nice place, a long way away—ruling Egypt is now that much simpler.

CYPRUS

③ SPEND QUALITY TIME TOGETHER

The Egyptian people are very happy about me coruling—my siblings less so. Ptolemy XIII decides to attack us, and Arsinoe joins in. But it gives Caesar and me the chance to spend some quality time together, barricaded inside the royal palace.

④ ALWAYS PUT YOUR LOVE FIRST

Being bombarded by my siblings' army starts to get boring, so Caesar sends for reinforcements from Rome (swoon). When Caesar's soldiers finally arrive, they chase Ptolemy and Arsinoe to the River Nile. Ptolemy tries to escape but his boat capsizes and he drowns (note to self—gold armor is too heavy to swim in). Sorry, not sorry.

⑤ MAKE THE MOST OF YOUR TIME APART

Caesar leaves Alexandria not long after the skirmish, but he leaves behind 3 legions of Roman soldiers for my protection. At last I can get some work done!

MY TOTAL REBRAND

So now that I've got my guy, and have power over the throne, it's time for a makeover...

I AM A GODDESS

One of the amazing things about ancient Egyptian culture is that you don't have to be dead to be a god! My siblings and I have always been considered gods, but it's time to shift things up a gear. I become the ultimate Egyptian goddess—Isis.

Umm, who's Isis?

Isis is the one wearing cow horns and a sun disc on her head. Isis was the wife of the god Osiris, who, a very long time ago, was the first king of Egypt (or at least that's what we like to believe).

uraeus crown—a cobra snake or snakes (most have 1 or 2 snakes, but mine has 3) rearing upright (Egyptian) = I am the ruler of Egypt

tripartite wig—for special occasions only, my wig is braided from real human hair and decorated with tassels and precious stones (Egyptian) = I descend from royalty

ankh—a symbol of life (Egyptian) = I will give life to Egypt

Why the cow horns?

So the myth goes that Osiris has a younger brother called Seth, who is jealous of Osiris and wants to be king. Seth murders Osiris, cuts his body into tiny pieces, scatters them around Egypt, and becomes king. Isis and her sister, Nephthys, collect all the body parts and bring Osiris back to life just long enough for them to have a baby together. The baby is Horus, who grows up determined to avenge his father's death. Horus and Seth have a long struggle during which Horus cuts off his own mother's head—stick with me... She survives and it gets replaced with a cow's head, which is why you often see Isis wearing cow horns. Phew!

GREEK–EGYPTIAN MASH-UP

Borrowing style tips from Isis is how I will endear myself to the Egyptian population. But I also need to keep my fellow Greeks happy—we are equally as proud of our own culture.

cornucopia—a horn filled with produce (Greek) = I will provide for my people

MY EVERYDAY LOOK

The wig is mostly for special occasions. For an everyday look, or when I'm visiting Caesar in Rome, I wear my hair in the "melon" hairstyle (so hot right now) with a uraeus headband.

TREND ALERT!

melon hairstyle—curly hair sectioned into waves and tied at the nape of the neck in a bun (Greek) = I am from the Ptolemaic Dynasty

MY SON, LITTLE CAESAR

When you're trying to rebrand yourself as the mother of a country, it really helps when you can show that you are a wonderful mother in real life.

LIKE FATHER, LIKE SON

It's after Caesar returns to Rome that I have our baby. What do I name him? Ptolemy of course! (Ptolemy XV Caesar, officially). Everyone calls him "Caesarion" though, which means "Little Caesar," after his dad.

BABY-FACED RULER

One of the advantages of having had a baby is that, according to tradition, I'm allowed to rule on Caesarion's behalf. At last, I no longer have to be officially married to one of my brothers—woohoo!

BTW, what happened to Ptolemy XIV?

A rumor goes round in 44 BCE that I have poisoned my own brother to give Caesarion a clear path to the throne. I have no comment...

HOLY MOTHER OF EGYPT!

To celebrate the birth of my first child, instead of a baby shower I decide to build a temple. I choose a site in Armant, near Thebes, which is where previous pharaohs built their temples.

I have drawings made on the walls—it's hard to tell if they're of me giving birth or Isis. Is that me breastfeeding Caesarion or Isis suckling Horus? The confusion is intentional and people get the message: I am the holy mother of Egypt.

Depressing side note: my temple stands for almost 2,000 years, but is destroyed in modern times, in 1861–63 —to make way for a sugar factory. Can you believe it?!

THE WRITING'S ON THE WALL

In case anyone hasn't got the message, I inscribe my full Egyptian name on the temple wall: "the female Horus, the great one, mistress of perfection, brilliant in counsel, Mistress of the Two Lands, Cleopatra Philopator."

GETTING THE WORD OUT

Without social media at my disposal, I have to find other ways of sharing my new look.

NO EXPENSE SPARED

As a world leader, I need to put a lot of thought and money into my appearance—literally. I have some coins made showing my everyday look on one side and a cornucopia on the other.

LET'S CRUISE!

Before Caesar has to go back to Rome, I make sure I am seen with the most powerful man in the world. We go on a luxurious cruise down the River Nile. Caesar brings his 400 ships—a fantastic show of power—and I sail on my favorite boat, *Thalamegos*. We can't NOT be seen.

GOING GLOBAL

Julius—bless him—takes me to Rome after Caesarion is born. He has a golden statue of me erected in the Temple of Venus Genetrix in Rome. Venus is the Roman goddess of love and the giver of life, so I'm in excellent company. I also put a statue in the Acropolis in Athens when I go there.

LUXURY IS MY MIDDLE NAME

It is important to display my wealth both to my subjects and to Julius Caesar. My boat says it all—it's over 295 ft long, 2 stories, has its own gardens, and has a roof terrace looking out onto the river (perfect for waving from). The dining room has 20 couches, and is decorated with ivory and gold. Lush.

MY BOYFRIEND IS ASSASSINATED

As it turns out, you can be too powerful.
Julius learns this the hard way...

POWER TRIP

Julius recently got promoted to dictator by the Roman senate—the government. The senators Cassius and Marcus Brutus think the power has gone to Caesar's head. They start a rumor that Caesar wants to be king of the Roman Republic. If there's one thing Romans hate, it's the idea of a monarchy.

MURDER ON THE SENATE FLOOR

On his way into a boring government meeting in 44 BCE, Caesar is attacked by a group of senators. They stab him 23 times—in broad daylight! Politics is dangerous.

I'M SINGLE AGAIN

So thanks to a bunch of jealous old senators, I am now widowed at the tender age of 36 and a single mother to baby Caesarion, who will never know his dad...

CHAOS REIGNS

Caesar's death causes all sorts of chaos in Rome because no one really knows who is supposed to be in charge. He is replaced by a triumvirate, or group of three rulers. They agree to jointly rule Italy and split the rest of the Roman Republic between them.

In Caesar's will, he names his 18-year-old grand-nephew as his adoptive heir. Octavian inherits his riches and takes over the western part of the Roman Republic.

MARK ANTONY

Greece, Turkey, Syria, and Egypt

OCTAVIAN

Spain, France, and Croatia

Mark Antony served Caesar as a general in the army and is a successful politician. He takes control of the east, which includes Egypt, and me!

LEPIDUS

North Africa

Lepidus is suspected of siding with Pompey, Julius Caesar's old enemy. He is assigned a very small territory in North Africa.

Italy

Egypt

But let's say Egypt is mine!

MY SECOND BOYFRIEND, MARK ANTONY

Generally I agree that you should never be friends with the people you work with. Unless you fall in love with them, that is.

A MEETING OF MINDS

Mark Antony invites me to a business meeting in Turkey. At first I say no—I'm a single mother with a country to run! But networking is important, so I agree—on the condition that we meet on board the *Thalamegos* (I want to make a good first impression). We have a very productive meeting and Mark Antony agrees to action the "removal" of my sister Arsinoe IV, who is exiled in his territory, in Ephesus. What? She's just so annoying!

THE GIFT OF LOVE

Finding the perfect gift for a world leader you're trying to impress is a delicate task. Mark Antony gifts me Cyprus—as in the Greek island (although technically it belonged to my family originally—just saying). I give him 200 naval ships to help solve the troubles he's having in Syria. That's when it hits me: I am in love with Mark Antony, and he is in love with me.

HONEYMOON BABIES

To cement our relationship, I give birth to Mark Antony's twins. We name them Alexander Helios (Greek for "the sun") and Cleopatra Selene ("the moon"). In the summer of 36 BCE we have another boy, who we call... Ptolemy! Ptolemy Philadelphus, to be precise.

A POLITICAL MARRIAGE

Mark Antony has a serious falling out with his fellow ruler Octavian (the Romans aren't too happy about the cities Antony keeps giving me). To smooth things over, they strike a deal—Mark Antony will give back the parts of Italy, Spain, and France he took. He will also marry Octavian's sister, Octavia, to unite their 2 families. Am I angry? Yes. Am I worried? Of course not!

PRESENTS FOR THE CHILDREN

To make up for all the time Antony spends away from me and the kids, he abandons Octavia and we have a massive party in the gymnasium. Mark Antony showers the children with gifts. He makes little Alexander Helios the king of Armenia, Media, and Parthia; his sister Cleopatra Selene gets Crete and Cyrene, and Ptolemy Philadelphus becomes the king of Syria and Cilicia. He is only 2!

EGYPT News

EXTRA!

ROME DECLARES WAR!

Mark Antony's extravagant gift giving attracts criticism in Rome. Because I am not his official wife, the tabloids assume I must be brainwashing him. They declare war—not on Mark Antony, but on ME!

MY UNTIMELY DEATH

The tale of my death starts with the Battle of Actium and ends with a snake bite.

THE BATTLE OF ACTIUM

The reason Rome declares war on me is because Mark Antony announces that Caesarion is Julius Caesar's heir (Caesar had said it was Octavian—oops...), and that Alexandria is the new capital of the Roman Republic. You can see why they'd be angry. The war could go either way: I have more men, but they are a bit of a rabble—Octavian's men are total PROS. With 60 ships in tow, we sail to our battleground: the Ionian Sea in Greece, near Actium.

KEEP OUT!

WE ACCEPT OUR LOSSES

Despite having joined forces, Mark Antony and I have to accept our losses. My entire fleet is burned, and Antony's soldiers take the side of Octavian. We jump ship and return to Alexandria. Mark Antony is so unhappy, he builds himself a temple to sulk in, called the Timonium—the royal equivalent of a man cave.

I TRY TO BRIBE MY WAY OUT

I try to patch things up with Octavian but none of my bribes work—not even the golden crown and throne I send him. So I threaten to take all of Egypt's treasures into my tomb and set fire to them. All this does is prompt Octavian to invade Alexandria—he is hugely in debt after all his warring and needs my money! This is when it starts to go wrong...

OUR FINAL EMBRACE

Mark Antony fights Octavian to defend Alexandria but loses. I hide in my tomb and send a fake message to Mark Antony, saying that I have died, in the hope that Octavian will leave us alone. Instead, Antony is so upset, he stabs himself in the stomach. I manage to get one last message to Antony to reassure him I'm actually alive. We are reunited in my tomb, but Mark Antony dies in my arms.

A TRAGIC END

In 30 BCE Octavian successfully takes over the royal palace. I would rather die than have him steal the Ptolemaic Dynasty from me. There are many rumors about how I actually die—my favorite one is that I arrange for a venomous snake to bite me. So long, beloved followers. It's been a blast.

NOW EVERYONE'S WRITING ABOUT ME

Just because I'm dead, it doesn't mean I can't still win friends and influence people.

"I hate the queen!" – Cicero
Letter to Atticus, 44 BCE

The Roman lawyer Cicero is one of the few people who write about me who is alive during my lifetime. According to a letter to his good friend Atticus, I am so arrogant, he doesn't want anything to do with me. I guess that explains why we're not friends.

"That deadly monster" – Horace
Odes, Book 1/37, 23 BCE

Tell me this—would you trust a poet who was prone to exaggeration to write a history book? Didn't think so. And yet it's Horace's dramatization of the final days of my life that sticks in everyone's mind. I'm not a monster plotting to ruin Rome—I'm much more ambitious. I want to the rule the world!

HORACE

CLEOPATRA

"There was sweetness in her voice" – Plutarch
Life of Antony, 2 CE

Despite having NEVER met me, the philosopher Plutarch is very impressed by my intellect and my ability to speak many languages. But his sources are dubious—he claims to have read the memoirs of my physician, Olympus, and says his grandfather had a friend who knew my cook…

"Egypt's shame" – Lucan
On the Civil War, Book 10, 60 CE

Epic poems are called that because they are epically long and wordy. In Lucan's epic about Caesar's battle with Pompey, he uses many words to describe me, including "insolent" and "vile." He even claims that I drugged Caesar to get him to like me. I think of him less as a poet, more as a troll.

"A woman of surpassing beauty ... with the power to subjugate everyone"
– Cassius Dio
Roman History, 200–222 CE

Cassius Dio is a senator who fancies himself as my "biographer." Dio claims I use witchcraft to make Antony choose me over Octavia— but I don't need supernatural powers to influence people. That's just girl power.

"Age cannot wither her" – William Shakespeare
Antony and Cleopatra, 1607

We all know the English playwright was no historian, but there's one thing that Shakespeare did get right about me—I'm gonna live forever. I am, after all, the goddess Isis, the Queen of Kings—Cleopatra!

My advice to all aspiring world leaders is this: ignore the haters and #make it happen. (Also, write your own history, which can be backed up with reliable sources.)

ALEXANDRIA SINKS INTO THE SEA

When I say Alexandria declines after my death, I mean it literally sinks into the sea.

EARTHQUAKE!!!

An earthquake and tsunami in 365 CE, and further earthquakes in the Middle Ages, cause the coast of Alexandria to subside, or sink, into the sea. The lighthouse topples over and the palace complex sinks 30 ft below the water's surface.

a black granite statue of a priest carrying an Osiris jar from my palace on Antirhodos Island

a marble statue of the Greek god Hermes from my palace

WATERY GRAVE

Our palaces remain under water until 1992, when French marine archaeologist Franck Goddio, together with the Egyptian Ministry of Antiquities, discovers more than 2,000 pieces of columns in Alexandria's harbor.

UNDERWATER TREASURES

Goddio's team make more than 3,500 dives to map the ancient city of Alexandria. Hidden under sand and sediment, they uncover temples, buildings, palaces, sphinxes, stelae, and statues, as well as ceramics, coins, pots, and jewelry.

a sphinx made from black granite representing my father, Ptolemy XII

Little Caesarion's sphinx statue made from granite

MY LEGEND LIVES ON

Rome may have wanted me dead, but its citizens love my style so much they help to turn me into a TOTAL LEGEND.

CLEOPATRA CRAZE

After Octavian (who becomes the first Roman emperor, Caesar Augustus) takes over Egypt, he refuses to put another Egyptian ruler on the throne—rude! But his Roman subjects love me so much, they start importing Egyptian objects to decorate their homes and temples. That's what I call sweet revenge.

THE NEED FOR NEEDLES

Everyone thinks the obelisks, or needles, by the ocean in Alexandria are mine: but they're not! When the Americans turn up in the 19th century, they steal the first "Cleopatra's Needle." Then the English turn up and take the other. Now I have a presence in both New York and London.

EGYPT Style

RULE like a QUEEN

GENUINE FAKES

Some canny Egyptians give old statues hairstyles like mine to cash in on the craze. They carve my personal cartouche into fake souvenirs to make them look genuine!

THE ROSETTA STONE

It may look like a lump of stone with tiny scribbles on it, but this is what makes ancient Egyptian culture go viral.

OFFICIAL NOTICE

The Rosetta Stone is an official notice, or decree, issued in 196 BCE by the Egyptian priests in Memphis. It basically says that Ptolemy V's rule over Egypt is legit.

It is copied onto multiple stone slabs called "stelae" (no photocopiers back then) and placed in temples in Egypt. To make sure EVERYONE gets the message, it is written out 3 times in 3 different scripts:

ANCIENT EGYPTIAN

During my family's reign, only priests know how to read and write hieroglyphics. They fall out of use entirely by 394 CE.

DEMOTIC SCRIPT

The native Egyptian script that everyday people use.

ANCIENT GREEK

The language my family uses and the official language of Alexandria and the Ptolemaic Dynasty.

What's Napoleon got to do with it?

The Rosetta Stone is discovered in 1799 by French soldiers in Napoleon Bonaparte's army during an attempt to conquer Egypt. By this time, all knowledge of Egyptian hieroglyphics is lost but scholars can still read ancient Greek. Hieroglyphics can now be decoded and everyone becomes obsessed with ancient Egypt.

MAP OF ALEXANDRIA

Welcome to my favorite city in the entire world! This shows how it looked during my lifetime (c. 70–30 BCE).

Pharos Lighthouse

GREAT HARBOR

MEDITERRANEAN SEA

Antirhodos Island
where I built my private palace

Timonium
Mark Antony's man cave

ISLAND OF PHAROS

Temple of Poseidon
(Greek god of the sea)

Heptastadium
The pier that joins the mainland to the island. In Greek it means "seven stadia," its measurement.

Port Buildings

Shipyard

PORT EUNOSTUS
(THE OLD PORT)

The Museion
where I spend all my time listening to scholars

I've drawn this with a little help from the Greek geographer Strabo. Archaeologists don't know where most of the famous buildings were—they'll be amazed when they see this!

Gate of the Moon

Serapeum
A temple to Serapis, the Greek/Egyptian god and protector of Alexandria.

Temple of Isis (an Egyptian mother goddess)

LOCHIAS POINT

Old Royal Palace
The buildings and gardens have views of the lighthouse, accessed by a private harbor.

Gate of the Sun (Canopic Gate)

Royal Harbor

Great Theater
where Julius Caesar hid from an angry mob

Gymnasium
where Ptolemy XI was unlucky enough to get murdered

Tomb of Alexander the Great
where Ptolemy I created an elaborate tomb for Alexander the Great—right in the center of town

CITY WALL

Cleopatra's Canal
This canal runs around the edge of the city into Lake Mareotis, which turns into the River Nile. It's named after me because I sailed my boats along it when I set out on my pleasure trips.

LAKE MAREOTIS

Glossary

ankh – a symbol that looks like a cross with a loop on top. Means "life"

archaeologist – someone who studies history by digging up objects from the ground and studying them

astronomer – a scientist who studies stars, planets, and outer space

Buchis bull – a sacred bull with a white body and a black face

cartouche – an oval surrounding a royal's name

catafalque – a burial chariot

coregent – joint ruler

cornucopia – an object shaped like a horn. Means "wealth"

dictator – a ruler who has absolute power and control

dynasty – a family of rulers who rule a country for generations

empire – a group of different countries that are controlled by one ruler (usually by force, to take money and possessions)

ginesthoi – a Greek word meaning "make it happen"

gymnasium – a building that was used for exercising, bathing, and learning

hieroglyphics –the picture symbols that were using for writing in ancient Egypt

legion – a very large group of Roman soldiers

obelisk – a stone pillar in the shape of a needle

oration – giving speeches

papyrus – a paper-like material made from the papyrus plant

pharaoh – the ruler in ancient Egypt

philosophy – the study of questions about the world and what it means to be a human

sarcophagus – a stone coffin

scribe – a person whose job it is to write out official documents by hand

senate – the government of the Roman Empire

sphinx – a mythical creature with a woman's head and a lion's body

stelae – stone slabs with writing or drawings carved into them

tripartite – something that has three parts

triumvirate – a group of three leaders

uraeus – a symbol showing an upright cobra snake or snakes. Means "I am the ruler of Egypt"

Roman numerals

Roman numerals are the numbers that were used by the ancient Romans. They're often used in the names of kings and queens, even when they aren't Roman. We royals often have family names, so the Roman numerals are a useful way to tell us all apart. You wouldn't want to learn about some other Cleopatra instead of me, Cleopatra VII, right?! Roman numerals are used for lots of other things, too, so they're totally a skill worth mastering. I told you I was queen of the geeks!

Roman numerals are specific letters and letter combinations that represent numbers. Here are the key Roman numerals:
I = 1
V = 5
X = 10
L = 50
C = 100
D = 500
M = 1,000

When 2 letters are combined, you add together the different letters to make a number, like this:
VI = 5 + 1 = 6

When the same letter is repeated several times in a row, you add them together:
XIII = 10 + 1 + 1 + 1 = 13

The same letter shouldn't be repeated more than 3 times in a row. Instead, when a smaller number is listed before a larger number, the smaller number is subtracted from the larger number. Got that? So instead of writing the number 4 as IIII, you write it as IV:
IV = 5 - 1 = 4

Now that you've mastered Roman numerals, the Roman Empire's putty in your hands!

Index

DR CHRIS NAUNTON is an Egyptologist and author from London, U.K., who is often on TV. He has written lots of books including *King Tutankhamun Tells All!*, *Searching for the Lost Tombs of Egypt*, and *Egyptologists' Notebooks*. He has been to Egypt more times than he can count.

GUILHERME KARSTEN is an illustrator from Blumenau, Brazil, who has won many prestigious awards for his artwork. He is the author and illustrator of *Aaahhh!* and has illustrated over 30 books for children including *King Tutankhamun Tells All!*

First published in 2022 in the United States of America by Thames & Hudson Inc., 500 Fifth Avenue, New York, New York 10110

ISBN 978-0-500-65256-5

Library of Congress Control Number 2021947710

Printed and bound in China by C&C Offset Printing Co. Ltd

MIX
Paper from responsible sources
FSC® C008047

Be the first to know about our new releases, exclusive content and author events by visiting
thamesandhudson.com
thamesandhudsonusa.com
thamesandhudson.com.au

Cleopatra was an impressive ruler, it's true. But have you read my story? You won't be able to put it down!

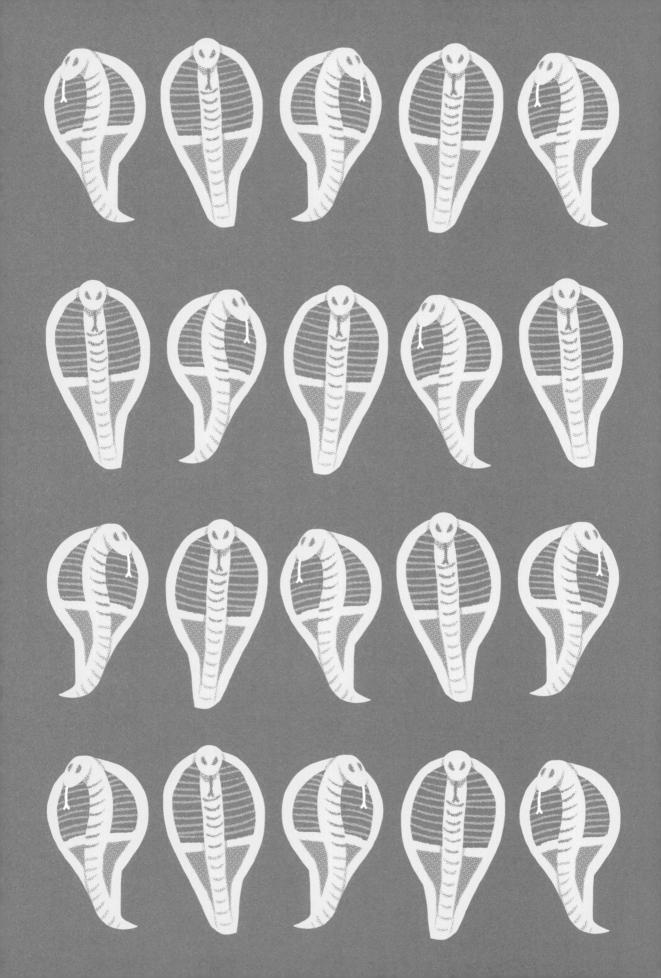